Wendy Hatcher served as a State Chaplain in the Mississippi prison system for over thirty years, beginning with the infamous Parchman Prison in the Delta and eventually becoming Head Chaplain at the state's newest facility. These stories and readings are for those serving time in prisons across the globe, as well as for those in the "free world" with an interest in life behind bars.

"Wendy Hatcher served as a moral compass for both staff and inmates in her role as Chaplain at two Mississippi prisons. She was a mentor, community servant, and continues to be a strong Christian. Her devotion to people, her wisdom, and her desire to serve God have earned her great credibility and respect. Through Wendy's efforts, she leads many people to the Lord and through her example, she teaches the true meaning of life."

Raymond Roberts, Warden
Eldorado Correctional Facility, Kansas

"My friend Wendy Hatcher has developed a wonderful resource that will encourage, challenge and strengthen you on your spiritual journey. It is practical, engaging and fast-paced, and if you take its messages to heart, it will change your relationship with God and your fellow man."

Chuck Colson,
Founder and Chairman
Prison Fellowship

Doing Time

Inspirational Readings from Life in Prison

by Wendy Hatcher

Delta Publishing
Seattle, Washington

ISBN 0-9779231-0-X

Designer: W. Leigh Borrou

Published in the U.S.
by *Delta Publishing*
a division of *Delta Imaging*
Seattle, Washington
www.deltaimaging.biz
Contact: doingtime@deltaimaging.biz
P.O. Box 25298
Federal Way, WA 98093

Doing Time

"Now listen, you say, today or tomorrow we will go to this or that city, spend a year there, carry on business and make money. Why, you do not even know what will happen tomorrow. What is your life? You are a mist that appears for a little while and then vanishes."

James 4: 13-14

As a prison chaplain, I was around thousands of men and women "doing time," as they described their prison sentences. Life stopped when the gate closed behind them. Living ended when the prison term began, and would resume only after release. Yet the years passed just the same.

We are all doing time! We all have an allotted amount. How much, we are not told, but the Bible tells us it is disappearing as steam. Anyone over fifty can attest to that.

It is not where the body is that counts. It is where the *heart* is – that part of us which is free to live *for* God, or in opposition to Him.

I have seen inmates continue to live as they did in the "free world", wasting precious years living in emptiness. I have also heard some say wistfully, *"Things will be different when I get out."* Yet, I have also seen those who achieved peace and purpose, in spite of the limitations of prison life. Jesus said, *"I have come that they may have life and have it to the full."* (John 10:10) He didn't exclude the elderly, the handicapped, the uneducated, or the poor. He didn't exclude the prisoners either.

Whether we are in humble surroundings or whether we are rich, whether we achieve fame or remain unknown, is of no consequence. When we come to Him in repentance and surrender, He will fill our lives with meaning.

Time, as we understand it, will quickly evaporate, but He will always be. The greatest need in time, wherever we spend it, is to know God.

For Further Thought ....

Psalm 39:5   "You have made my days a mere handbreath; the span of my years as nothing before you. Each man's life is but a breath."

Matthew 22: 37-39   "Jesus replied: 'Love the Lord your God with all your heart and with all your soul and with all your mind. And the second is like it: 'Love your neighbor as yourself.' "

WHAT ARE THESE VERSES SAYING ABOUT THE PRIORITIES OF LIFE?

MY NOTES:

_____

_____

_____

_____

_____

_____

_____

_____

_____

_____

_____

_____

_____

_____

_____

_____

_____

_____

_____

_____

_____

_____

Being

"God made Him who had no sin to be sin for us, so that we might become the righteousness of God."
2nd Corinthians 5:21

 We look at those who have committed what society calls "heinous" crimes (or sins) and think that the perpetrators are too evil to merit God's forgiveness. On the other hand, many who were privileged to grow up in nice families with parents or society, who taught them to be decent, law-abiding citizens, whose greatest illegal activity is a speeding ticket, often see no need of God's forgiveness.

Jesus death was for all mankind because we all have that nature which causes us to commit sin (or crimes). As Oswald Chambers said in his book, *My Utmost For His Highest,* "sin is not wrong doing but wrong being."

I recently heard a very important politician, who was trying to gain the Christian vote, quote what he called the most important commandments, "You shall love the Lord your God with all heart, with all your soul and with all your strength, and your neighbor as yourself." Absolutely true. He then interpreted it to mean that everything will be alright if we just have more love for everyone. What he didn't seem to understand is that we cannot just determine to develop that kind of love. Our sinful nature must be changed, and it can only be changed as we accept what Christ did on the cross. It is His love that makes the difference.

The most hardened criminal, and the sweetest little old lady you know, are all equally in need of the "washing away" of our sin nature. We must all come to Him admitting our need of that "bath."

For Further Thought ....

Exodus 20 :3-17   "You shall have no other Gods before me."

"You shall not make for yourself an idol in the form of anything in heaven above or on the earth beneath or in the waters below. You shall not bow down to them or worship them; for I, the Lord your God , am a jealous God, punishing the children for the sin of the fathers to the third and fourth generation of those who hate me, but showing love to a thousand generations of those who love me and keep my commandments."

"You shall not misuse the name of the Lord your God, for the Lord will not hold anyone guiltless who misuses His name."

"Remember the Sabbath day by keeping it holy. Six days you shall labor and do all your work, but the seventh day is a Sabbath to the Lord your God. On it you shall not do any work, neither you , nor your son or daughter, nor your manservant or maidservant, nor your animals, nor the alien within your gates. For in six days the Lord made the heavens and the earth, the sea, and all that is in them, but He rested on the seventh day. Therefore the Lord blessed the Sabbath day and made it holy."

"Honor your father and your mother, so that you may live long in the land the Lord your God is giving you."

"You shall not murder."

"You shall not commit adultery."

9

"You shall not steal."

"You shall not give false testimony against your neighbor."

"You shall not covet your neighbor's house. You shall not covet your neighbor's wife, or his manservant or maidservant, his ox or donkey, or anything that belongs to your neighbor."

IS IT POSSIBLE TO KEEP THE TEN COMMANDMENTS PERFECTLY?

Jeremiah 17:9   "The heart is deceitful beyond all things, and beyond cure. Who can understand it?"

WHAT IS THIS VERSE TEACHING US ABOUT OUR TENDENCY TO SIN?

MY NOTES:

_____
_____
_____
_____
_____
_____
_____
_____
_____
_____
_____
_____
_____
_____
_____
_____
_____
_____
_____
_____

Sin Pie

"And no wonder, for Satan himself masquerades as an
angel of light."
II Corinthians 11:14

We had the Governor of the state of Mississippi visit the prison for lunch one day. It was a very special event for the prison, the inmates, and the staff.

The inmate helpers at the Chaplains' department helped to prepare a sumptuous meal, culminating in a dessert we called "sin pie." The Governor was delighted with the pie and asked what it was. After being told what it was called, he asked why we chose that name for something so delicious. I replied, *"Governor, the pie is just like sin. In the beginning, it is usually so good and so much fun, but in the end it bites us."* He still didn't quite get it, so I elaborated, *"This pie is full of calories and fat and it is not good for us. If we eat enough of it, we will destroy our health."* Sin is like that!

Why are our prisons and jails so full of people involved in drug and alcohol-related crimes? Mainly because what at first seemed fun and satisfying or self-gratifying later turned into an addiction, resulting in all the crimes associated with substance abuse.

When Satan comes to us disguised as something delicious, we must think of the consequences.

For Further Thought ....

James 1:14-15 *"Each one is tempted when, by his own evil desire, he is dragged away and enticed. Then after desire has conceived, it gives birth to sin, and sin, when it is full-grown, gives birth to death."*

Job 20:12-14 *"Though evil is sweet in his mouth and he hides it under his tongue, though he cannot bear to let it go and keeps it in his mouth, yet his food will turn sour in his stomach; it will become the venom of serpents within him."*

WHAT IS THE END RESULT OF SIN?

MY NOTES:

_____
_____
_____
_____
_____
_____
_____
_____
_____
_____
_____
_____
_____
_____
_____
_____

"SON" Shine

*"He will bring to light what is hidden in darkness and will
expose the motives of men's hearts."*
1 Corinthians 4:5b

The inevitable grime of Summer dust and insects had encrusted the windows of our office at the prison. The furniture needed a shine, and there were signs of general neglect. One of my inmate assistants decided it all needed "a good clean." She scrubbed and polished with great vigor and enthusiasm.

When windows sparkled and the desks shone, she was justifiably proud of her labor.

However, as the day continued and the afternoon sun placed its spotlight on the room, the imperfections began to show. A smear here, a spot missed; undiscovered spider webs now quite apparent; rubber heel marks on the floors. When that great light exposed the reality, all her sincere efforts seemed insignificant. She had done all she could do, but it just wasn't enough. She just couldn't see it all without the light.

Likewise we can turn over new leaves, make New Years' resolutions, get educated, spend hours with the psychiatrist, wear the right clothes, read our Bibles, attend church, and feel proud of the results – until the Son shines upon us! We then discover we didn't do such a good job after all.

The best time to clean the room is to wait until the sun shines directly on it. The only time to be cleansed from sin is when what we really are is exposed by the Son of God – not before. Then He will clean us perfectly!

For Further Thought ....

Luke 11:39 "Then the Lord said to him, 'Now then, you Pharisees clean the outside of the cup and dish, but inside you are full of greed and wickedness.'"
THE PHARISEES THOUGHT THEY LIVED GOOD, CLEAN LIVES, BUT JESUS KNEW THE TRUTH. WHAT ABOUT US?

John 3:20 "Everyone who does evil hates the light, and will not come into the light, for fear that his deeds will be exposed."
WHAT HAPPENS WHEN WE ALLOW GOD TO EXPOSE OUR SIN?

MY NOTES:

_____
_____
_____
_____
_____
_____
_____
_____
_____
_____
_____
_____
_____
_____
_____
_____
_____
_____

Snow

*"Cleanse me with hyssop and I will be clean, wash
me and I will be whiter than snow."*
Psalm 51:7

We had snow in the Mississippi Delta one year, enough to make snowmen and slide down the levee or an Indian mound. At the prison we excitedly watched it from offices and guard towers. Even in isolated cells, eager faces could be seen peering through narrow windows, enthralled with the delicate lace from the skies. No doubt we all had childhood memories of "snow days."

The inmates were locked down, and the staff, except for essential personnel, were sent home. After all, we aren't prepared for the "white stuff" in Mississippi, and we certainly don't know how to drive in it!

We awakened the next morning to a blanket of several inches and, to the delight of children, no school. I cautiously drove the almost deserted highways, arriving at the prison to be astonished and delighted at the beauty I beheld. The dreary place was transformed. With the snow covering them. the dilapidated buildings had become as picturesque as chalets. The normally dusty or muddy "yards" and roads were sparkling and took me back to distant memories of a trip to Switzerland. I never imagined the place could look so enchanting.

The ugly was still there, but it was completely covered in white. *"Only God can do that."* I told the gate officer.

Of course, in a day or two, the snow melted and the reality of a dismal prison reappeared. I had been reminded, however, that God permanently transforms our "ugly" when we allow the Son of God to cover our sin with His purity. Only God can do that!

17

For Further Thought ....

Psalm 51:7 *"Cleanse me with hyssop, and I will be clean; wash
me, and I will be whiter than snow".*
WHO CLEANSES AND WASHES?
(Note: hyssop was for ritual cleansing)

Isaiah 1:18 *"Come now, let us reason together, says the Lord.
Though your sins are like scarlet, they shall be white as snow.
Though they are red as crimson, they shall be like wool."*
*SIN IS USUALLY CALLED BLACK. HOW DOES IT BECOME
WHITE? HOW IS SIN COVERED?*

MY NOTES:

_____
_____
_____
_____
_____
_____
_____
_____
_____
_____
_____
_____
_____
_____
_____
_____
_____
_____
_____
_____
_____

His Sheep

*"My sheep listen to my voice; I know them and
they follow me."*
John 10:27

As the spiritual leader of a prison, a chaplain struggles to protect the residents from the influence of false teaching, while still allowing them access to the religious instruction of their choice. This is not only mandated by State Government, it is an American right – even in prison.

However, some groups cause great confusion and strife with their claims to be the *only* Christians. They continue to infiltrate prisons, bringing misery to chaplains and problems to security. They often destroy the peace which Christian inmates have found.

After an extremely unpleasant battle with my superiors, I was once ordered to allow such a group to conduct weekly meetings at the prison. I lay awake at night fretting over the damage being done by them, greatly disturbed that the new Christians were troubled and non-Christians were being deceived. *"What can I do to protect them, Lord?"* I urgently entreated.

The answer didn't come - but that still, small, voice asked a question. *"Whose sheep are they?"*
"Oops, I forgot, Lord."

Nothing can snatch God's people out of His hands, if they truly belong to Him. No earthly, or unearthly, power can separate us from His love and protection. I understood that truth for myself, having been rescued early in my Christian life from all kinds of dangers, including false teaching. I was now arrogantly assuming that I had to take care of *my* babies.

How comforting it is to know that He will protect us.

For Further Thought ....

Matthew 7:15 "Watch out for false prophets. They come to you in sheep's clothing, but inwardly they are ferocious wolves.

2nd Timothy 2:15 "Do your best to present yourself to God as one approved, a workman who does not need to be ashamed and one who correctly handles the Word of Truth."

IF WE ARE TO WATCH OUT FOR A FALSE PROPHET, HOW DO WE RECOGNIZE ONE?

MY NOTES:

Tornado

"Preach the Word; be prepared in season and out of season...."
2nd Timothy 4:2a

Tornado watches are frequent in the Mississippi Delta, and the prisons warn when a tornado is imminent. On the occasions when an alert is given, prison authorities must be prepared with a plan of action.

When a "watch" or a "warning" is sounded, radios are carefully monitored and eyes anxiously scan the skies. As a lock-down comes into effect, all inmates are sent to their buildings.

On one such occasion, as I was returning to the relative safety of a building, I encountered a worried-looking security officer. After exchanging concerns about the impending storm, I then asked him, *"Where you gonna go if you blow?"* *"Aw, chaplain,"* he responded, *"you never miss an opportunity do you?"* This was a casual moment, of course, but truly we must continue to remind people that life isn't guaranteed beyond the moment.

Think of those you know who have died "unexpectedly." Did 36-year-old Bobby even consider his life would suddenly end in a car wreck? Did seemingly healthy Joyce expect to have a fatal heart-attack? What about 16-year-old Tim drowning in a boating accident? Were they ready?

For Further Thought ....

Jeremiah 22: 21 "I warned you when you felt secure, but you said 'I will not listen.' This has been your way from your youth; you have not obeyed me."
WHEN HAVE YOU FAILED TO LISTEN TO GOOD ADVICE?

WHAT DOES IT MEAN TO BE "ON GUARD AND ALERT?"

Proverbs 27:1 "Do not boast about tomorrow, for you do not know what a day may bring forth"
DO WE FEEL TOO SAFE?

MY NOTES:

_____

_____

_____

_____

_____

_____

_____

_____

_____

_____

_____

_____

_____

_____

_____

_____

_____

_____

_____

Choices

"Choose for yourselves this day whom you will serve....."
Joshua 24:15b

The incarcerated are told when to go to bed, when to get up, what time to eat, what to wear, how to wear it. They go outside for fresh air when permitted and they are limited as to what they may do and with whom they associate. Jobs are assigned, not chosen. Recreation and religious activities are confined to certain areas and designated times. All privileges are subject to change without explanation. Freedom of choice is practically nil.

Sinful choices, of course, are what bring the consequences of prison sentences, but it is still frustrating for adults. On one occasion, in response to a complaining Christian inmate, I reminded him, *"You still have the most important choices available. You still have the right to choose to obey both God's and mans' rules. You can decide to show God's love to the unlovely. You can keep your mind pure by thinking thoughts that are lovely and holy instead of filling it with the trash that is so readily available, even in prison. You can smile. You can bless those who persecute you. You can be a positive influence in this negative community. Never forget, no one can stop you from praying."*

Whether we have few or many choices, we must still choose to serve Him daily.

For Further Thought ....

Luke 10:38-42   "As Jesus and His disciples were on their way, He came to a village where a woman named Martha opened her home to him. She had a sister called Mary, who sat at the Lord's feet listening to what He said. But Martha was distracted by all the preparations that had to be made.
She came to him and asked, 'Lord, don't you care that my sister has left me to do the work by myself?
Tell her to help me.'
'Martha, Martha,' the Lord answered, 'you are worried and upset about many things. But only one thing is needed. Mary has chosen what is better, and it will not be taken away from her.'"

MY NOTES:

_____

_____

_____

_____

_____

_____

_____

_____

_____

_____

_____

_____

_____

_____

_____

_____

_____

_____

Excuses

"If anyone is in Christ he is a new creation, the old has gone, the new is come."
II Corinthians 5:17

We often use our upbringing, lack of education, or poverty as the reason for present behavior. *"My parents didn't love me, therefore I am selfish and hateful." "I didn't have 'stuff' like other kids, so I stole to get it." "Everyone else was doing it, why not me?"*

It is true that our past shapes our behavior, but we must not allow the past to continue to control it. When we stand before God, we will not be able to blame others for what we are, because He tells us we are without excuse. (Romans 1:20)

Does that mean there is no hope? Yes, there is hope. Beginning today, we can be changed immediately, so that whatever our background, whatever our crime, we can instantly be altered. Most likely it won't get us out of our present circumstances. But who we are - wherever we are - will be dramatically transformed.

Don't know how to accomplish that? Give as much of yourself as you can to as much of God as you understand, right now. Ask Jesus to forgive your past and grant you a brand new future. If you are in prison, take advantage of whatever is offered in there; ask to see a Christian chaplain or minister; request a Bible and pray to God for understanding of it.

For Further Thought ....

John 3:3   Jesus declared, "I tell you the truth, no one can see the Kingdom of God unless he is born again."

BEING BORN AGAIN IS A NEW START. AFTER READING THE DEVOTIONAL , WHAT DO YOU THINK JESUS MEANS BY THIS?

MY NOTES:

_____

_____

_____

_____

_____

_____

_____

_____

_____

_____

_____

_____

_____

_____

_____

_____

_____

_____

_____

_____

_____

_____

TIME FLIES

"A cheerful heart is good medicine, but a crushed spirit dries up the bones."
Proverbs 17:22a

A visiting preacher, speaking to a large congregation of inmates in the prison chapel one day, was concerned to stay within his allotted time. He paused briefly to ask, *"How much time do I have?"*

One inmate, not missing a beat, shouted *"I don't know about you, preacher, but I have to go in eighty years."* There was laughter and a cheer as others joined in, *"twenty years ... ten years ... five years. Don't worry, we're not going anywhere."*

Humor, in a prison? I've seen a joke diffuse a volatile situation; a smile brighten the gloom; a kind word bring a positive response.

On another occasion, where five hundred men were gathered in a chapel service in the prison gym, a thunderstorm knocked out some lights. What could have been a difficult or dangerous situation, became a happy event as someone led in the hymn *"I'll Fly Away."*

Certainly life in a prison community can be described in negative terms, but a sense of humor and a bright countenance do make a positive difference.

For Further Thought ....

Proverbs 12:25   *"An anxious heart weighs a man down, but a kind word cheers him up."*

Proverbs 15:13   *"A happy heart makes a face cheerful, but heartache crushes the spirit."*

Proverbs 15:15 *"All the days of the oppressed are wretched, but a cheerful heart has a continual feast."*

HOW DO OUR ATTITUDES AFFECT OTHERS?

Phillipians 4:4   *"Rejoice in the Lord always. I will say again, rejoice."*

PAUL WAS IN PRISON WHEN HE WROTE THIS. HOW DO YOU THINK HE MANAGED TO REJOICE?

MY NOTES:

_____

_____

_____

_____

_____

_____

_____

_____

_____

_____

_____

_____

_____

_____

_____

_____

_____

_____

_____

Baa - Baa

"The Lord is my Shepherd, I shall not want"
Psalm 23:1

This most familiar of Psalms has comforted millions through the ages. Anyone with a Sunday School background can quote this verse. It is the most often used Scripture during times of deep trouble.

As the sheep are totally dependent upon the shepherd for their protection, food and water, so are people unable to take care of themselves spiritually.

Do the sheep know they cannot make it alone? Are they conscious of danger around them? Not really. They are stupid. The shepherd must constantly watch out for them. We human beings are so sure of our ability to take care of ourselves that we ignore our Heavenly Shepherd until we find ourselves in situations we cannot handle.

When prison is our place of need, we either run around in circles trying to find a way out of our troubles, or we tuck our hind legs under and give up. What pitiful sheep we are. Our Shepherd will carry us back to His flock and care for us if we will but "bleat" for Him.

33

MY NOTES:

For Further Thought ....

Read all of Psalm 23 "The Lord is my shepherd, I shall not want. He makes me lie down in green pastures. He restores my soul. He guides me in paths of righteousness, for His names sake. Even though I walk through the valley of the shadow of death, I will fear no evil, for You are with me. Your rod and Your staff, they comfort me. You prepare a table before me in the presence of my enemies. You anoint my head with oil; my cup overflows. Surely goodness and love will follow me all the days of my life, and I will dwell in the house of the Lord forever."

THINK ABOUT THE HELPLESSNESS OF SHEEP.

Isaiah 53:6 "We all, like sheep, have gone astray; each of us has turned to his own way; and the Lord has laid on Him the iniquity of us all."

HOW ARE PEOPLE LIKE SHEEP? IS IT TRUE WE HAVE ALL GONE ASTRAY?

Obeying God

"How could I do such a wicked thing and sin against God?"
Genesis 39:9b

Joseph, the youngest son of a wealthy man, was sold into slavery by his jealous brothers and became a slave to a powerful man. The owner's wife was determined to seduce this handsome young man.

Was Joseph tempted to have a sexual encounter with his master's wife? Joseph was completely trusted by Potipher, his master, who had given him a good "catch[1]." But he was a slave and had no freedom to find a wife of his own. What do you think?

Can we use our imagination to read what he might have thought as she continually tried to seduce him:

She's my mistress, how can I refuse?
I need to keep her happy with me.
I will be able to do more for others if she
is on my side.
This is a perfectly natural thing to do.
God wants me to be happy.
I've earned some fun.
She will have me punished if I refuse.

He did refuse, and she did have him thrown in prison, where he remained for several years.

How could he overcome the incredible temptation? How did he resist trying to justify that some sin is okay? By putting obedience to God ahead of his own desires and acknowledging that ALL sin is against God.

1. *Catch = Job or Position*

For Further Thought ....

Psalm 51: 3 & 4   "For I know my transgressions and my sin is always before me.   Against you, you only, have I sinned and done what is evil in your sight."
HAVE YOU EVER THOUGHT YOUR SIN WAS ONLY AGAINST PEOPLE?

1st Samuel 15:24   "Then Saul said to Samuel, 'I have sinned. I violated the Lord's command and your instructions.   I was afraid of the people and so I gave in to them.'"
WAS SAUL MORE AFRAID OF PEOPLE OR GOD?

MY NOTES:

_____
_____
_____
_____
_____
_____
_____
_____
_____
_____
_____
_____
_____
_____
_____
_____
_____
_____
_____
_____

MY NOTES:

Fruit

"By their fruit you will recognize them."
Matthew 7:15

What in the world did Jesus mean when he said that we would recognize the real people of God by their "fruit?" Does the guy in the next rack[1], who claims to be a Christian, grow grapes in his ears? If he did he would probably get thrown in solitary for growing the means to make "buck"[2]. No, Jesus was saying that if a person knows Him, there will be evidence of it in that person's life.

Because I don't recognize one tree from another, I have to see the apples before I know it is an apple tree. It is the same with people. If the love for Christ and a desire to become more like Him is not evident in a life, we cannot be sure. In the book of 1st John, Chapter Two, the Apostle John says much about the "fruit" that will grow when someone belongs to Christ. It is summed up in Verse Six with the words, *"Whoever claims to live in Him must walk as Jesus did."*

To tell someone we are a Christian is not sufficient proof. We must show the "fruit" of belonging to Him.

---

1. *Rack: bed*
2. *Buck: homemade alcohol*

For Further Thought ....

Luke 6:43-45 *"No good tree bears bad fruit, nor does a bad tree bear good fruit. Each tree is recognized by its own fruit. People do not pick fruit from thorn bushes, or grapes from briars. The good man brings good things out of the good stored up in his heart. For out of the overflow of his heart his mouth speaks."*
CAN YOU THINK OF SOMEONE WHO PRODUCES "GOOD FRUIT?"

Galatians 5:22 & 23 *"But the fruit of the spirit is love, joy, peace, kindness, goodness, faithfulness, gentleness and self-control. Against such things there is no law."*
WHAT ARE SOME WAYS WE CAN SHOW THE FRUIT OF BELONGING TO JESUS?

MY NOTES:

Waiting Father

"Father, I have sinned against heaven and against you."
Luke 15:18

Jesus tells the story of a young man who walked away from the comfort and security of his father's home because he wanted to do his own thing. I'm sure he had lots of friends to help him spend his money – until it was gone. You can bet the friends left when the money left! Apparently they didn't stay around when trouble came. They were certainly gone when he was hungry enough to want to eat pigs' slop!

Is prison your pig sty? How often do you remember the family you left behind in your search for something better? How often do you think about the good free-world food that is now only a dream? How often do you wish you had stayed at home?

Why do we settle for a temporary thrill when God's best is available?

The young man came to his senses in that pig sty. He went home, willing to be anything his Dad wanted, but he didn't expect to be well-received.

His Dad was waiting for him with a big hug when he finally came home.

Our Heavenly Father will receive us with arms open wide when we come to Him admitting we have been wrong.

What a celebration He has ready!

For Further Thought ....

Luke 15: 4-6   "Suppose one of you had a hundred sheep and loses one of them. Does he not leave the ninety-nine in the open country and go after the lost sheep until he finds it? And when he finds it he puts it on his shoulders and goes home. Then he calls his friends and neighbors together and says, 'rejoice with me; I have found my lost sheep.'"
HOW IMPORTANT ARE WE TO GOD?

Luke 15: 8-10   "... or suppose a woman has ten silver coins and loses one. Does she not light a lamp, sweep the house and search carefully until she finds it? And when she finds it, she calls her friends and neighbors together and says 're-joice with me; I have found my lost coin.' In the same way, I tell you, there is rejoicing in the presence of the angels of God, over one sinner who repents."
WHAT MAKES GOD AND THE ANGELS REJOICE?

MY NOTES:

Singing In Max

There was usually a great deal of commotion in Women's Maximum Security. It was depressing to listen to the screams and profanity. Added to all that was the banging of fists on the communication system because officers were ignoring the appeals for help. Locked away from physical contact with each other, these women were going to talk, even if it meant shouting.

What could I tell the girls to alleviate some of their frustration? I thought of Paul and Silas in prison, accused of trying to cause a riot because they were preaching about Jesus. What did they do?

"Why don't you try singing together?" I suggested one day. It will remind you of Jesus and, besides, it will blow the minds of your officers.

They did! And it did! They all joined in to sing, "This is the day, this is the day, this is the day that the Lord has made."

It sure brightened up the cell block!

For Further Thought ....

Psalm 149:1   "Praise to the Lord. Sing to the Lord a new
song, His praise in the assembly of the saints."

Psalm 108:1   "My heart is steadfast, O God; I will sing and
make music with all my soul."
WHAT DO THESE AND MANY OTHER PSALMS
ENCOURAGE US TO DO?

MY NOTES:

_____

_____

_____

_____

_____

_____

_____

_____

_____

_____

_____

_____

_____

_____

_____

_____

_____

_____

_____

_____

_____

Follow Me

"Follow my example, as I follow the example of Christ."
1ˢᵗ Corinthians 11:1(b)

We have all heard voices telling us to "follow me" and often we have listened and done just that. Follow me as I commit this crime; follow me to the dope dealer; follow me to the casino; follow me in my rebellion. In the end it was "follow me to prison."

Michael was following his buddies when they attacked a teen-age girl. He was innocent of the actual molestation, but he was, nevertheless, with them. His associations resulted in a lot of time behind bars. He followed the wrong crowd. "I even *became* the wrong crowd," he told me one day.

Michael was "fitting in" with his buddies, but the consequences were painful. It was in prison, serving a long sentence, that he made the decision to follow Jesus Christ. Although it wasn't always easy, the rewards were satisfying and eternal.

When we respond to Jesus' invitation to follow Him, we are sometimes led into difficult situations. But He will never encourage us to sin and we will always have peace as we obey His directions.

For Further Thought ....

1 Corinthians 15: 33 "Do not be misled: Bad company corrupts good character."

Proverbs 22:24 & 25   "Do not make friends with a hot-tempered man, do not associate with one easily angered, or you may learn his ways and get yourself ensnared."

WHAT DO THESE SCRIPTURES TEACH US ABOUT OUR ASSOCIATIONS?

MY NOTES:

_____

_____

_____

_____

_____

_____

_____

_____

_____

_____

_____

_____

_____

_____

_____

_____

_____

_____

Set Free

"If the Son sets you free you will be free indeed."
John 8:36

James was assigned to help build the new prison chapel. In and out of prisons for most of his adult life because of alcohol addiction and related crimes, he was, nevertheless, hard-working and loyal to the Chaplains' Department. He was my friend. He was also totally uninterested in spiritual matters. If I tried to talk to him about new life in Jesus he would always change the subject.

Another of his addictions, tobacco, eventually caused him to suffer with lung cancer, experiencing great pain. Because of the kindness of an official, he was allowed to remain with us in the Chaplains' department where he finally understood his need of a Savior. He surrendered his life to Jesus.

I remember the day that James, now in a wheel chair, spoke to a group of touring teenagers. With tears streaming down his cheeks he told them, "Don't wait as long as I did to give your lives to Jesus. Don't waste your years thinking there is happiness in anything or anyone else."

He died one day in a prison dorm surrounded by Christian brothers. No more incarceration for James. That day he left prison for the last time to be with his friend, Jesus,
for eternity.

For Further Thought ....

John 8:34 *"Jesus said, 'I tell you the truth, everyone who sins is a slave to sin.'"*
2 Corinthians 3:17 *"Now the Lord is the spirit, and where the spirit of the Lord is there is freedom."*

HOW CAN SOMEONE IN PRISON STILL BE FREE?

MY NOTES:

_____
_____
_____
_____
_____
_____
_____
_____
_____
_____
_____
_____
_____
_____
_____
_____
_____
_____
_____
_____
_____
_____

Being Important

"But whatever was to my profit, I now consider loss
for the sake of Christ."
Philippians 3:7

"Edsel" was a floor-walker in B building. "Edsel" was rather simple. Most people ridiculed Edsel, but he didn't care because he had keys – a lot of them – hanging on his belt. He had special permission to have them. He was the only inmate I ever saw with keys. He strutted with them, and rattled them, and showed them to anyone indicating interest. They didn't open anything, of course. They were quite useless!

It was always rather sad to me, because I understood Edsel's real need. He wanted to be important; he wanted to be somebody. Don't we all? There is that desire to be special and needed in all of us. We fill our lives with all sorts of useless stuff and activity just to gain attention.

What we use to achieve recognition will no longer be necessary when we find fulfillment in knowing we are special to God.

For Further Thought ....

Read Philippians 3:7 "But whatever was to my profit I now consider loss for the sake of Christ. What is more, I consider everything a loss compared to the surpassing greatness of knowing Christ Jesus my Lord, for whose sake I have lost all things. I consider them rubbish, that I may gain Christ and be found in Him......"

WHAT DOES PAUL SAY ABOUT ALL THE THINGS THAT ONCE MADE HIM IMPORTANT?

Luke 14:33 "In the same way, any of you who does not give up everything he has cannot be my disciples."

DID JESUS MEAN EDSEL HAD TO GIVE UP HIS KEYS, OR THE PRIDE HE HAD IN THEM?

MY NOTES:

_____
_____
_____
_____
_____
_____
_____
_____
_____
_____
_____
_____
_____
_____
_____
_____

Good Example

"We are therefore Christ's ambassadors, as though God were making his appeal through us."
2nd Corinthians 5:20

Before we raised the money to build a chapel, with adjoining Chaplains' offices, the Department was constantly moving. It was stressful and frustrating, but I also saw the benefits.

On one occasion we were relocated into an area known to be a hot-bed of corruption. While I was somewhat irritated with the location, my Christian inmate assistants were eager to influence this area for Christ.

Within just weeks these dedicated Christian Trustees changed the atmosphere, not only with their refusal to participate in the criminal behavior, but with their obedience to rules and their constant message that Jesus is Lord.

They understood their role as Ambassadors of another Kingdom. These men represented their King so positively that many more prisoners were brought into His Kingdom, and those who did not change their allegiance were certainly subdued.

For Further Thought ....

2nd Corinthians 5:18-20 "All this is through God who reconciled us to Himself through Christ, and gave us the ministry of reconciliation; that God was reconciling the world to himself in Christ, not counting men's sins against them. And He has committed to us the message of reconciliation. We are, therefore, ambassadors as though God were making His appeal through us."

WHAT IS AN AMBASSADOR AND WHAT IS THE MESSAGE THAT WE, AS AMBASSADORS FOR CHRIST, BRING TO THOSE AROUND US?

Ephesians 6:19-20 "Pray also for me, that whenever I open my mouth, words may be given me so that I will fearlessly make known the mystery of the gospel, for which I am an ambassador in chains. Pray that I may declare it fearlessly, as I should."

KNOWING THAT PAUL WAS IN PRISON WHEN HE SAID THESE WORDS, HOW DO YOU REACT? CAN YOU BE AN AMBASSADOR FOR CHRIST?

MY NOTES:

Recidivism

"As a dog returns to its vomit, so a fool repeats his folly."
Proverbs 26:11

Recidivism is a big word we use to describe the criminal who returns to prison with another sentence. The dictionary describes a recidivist as "one who relapses into former behavior."

To the many who returned to the State receiving Center, I often asked, *"Oh, you must like it here?"* Of course I never expected a positive reply. Excuses usually went something like this:

"They were out to get me."
"I didn't do anything."
"They wouldn't give me work."
"Wrong place, wrong time."

For the most part these were not honest answers.

Some admitted, *"I messed up. I didn't take God with me."* The answer was quite simple: *"You flunked the test, now you will have to take it over."* The State is not forgiving.

The good news is that God *is* merciful and forgiving. The sobering news is that He requires repentance, which means we must stop trying to justify, and we must turn away from our sins.

For Further Thought ....

John 15: 22 *"If I had not come and spoken to them, they would not be guilty of sin. Now, however, they have no excuse for their sin."*

HOW DOES JESUS DESTROY OUR EXCUSES?

1st John 1:8 *"If we claim to be without sin, we deceive ourselves and the truth is not in us."*

WHO ARE WE TRYING TO FOOL WHEN WE SAY IT'S NOT OUR FAULT?

MY NOTES:

_____

_____

_____

_____

_____

_____

_____

_____

_____

_____

_____

_____

_____

_____

_____

_____

Going

"Then Jesus came to them and said, 'All authority in heaven and earth has been given to me. Therefore go and make disciples of all nations, baptizing them in the name of the Father and of the Son and of the Holy Spirit.'"
Matthew 28:18-19

Is it possible to live in a 6x9 cell and *"go into all the world?"* If you are in prison, you may be in despair of obeying God in this area.

Obviously "going" doesn't always mean running to the car or airplane to participate in a mission trip. It isn't even limited to visiting in the neighborhood or testifying in a church. If that were so, the elderly and handicapped would be excluded.

I am beginning to understand, as I become older and less able to rush around, that "going" can be simply "being." Being what He wants me to be where I am.

We have many examples of the early Christians "going" in prisons far worse than those we encounter in America today. The Apostle Paul wrote letters that later became part of the Bible while he was in prison, and he witnessed about God's love to his guards.

Wherever we have contact with other human beings, we can be part of the "go and teach others," by allowing Jesus to show Himself through us. A cheerful countenance to those who guard you, appreciation for the one who brings you food, a kind word to other inmates when the opportunity occurs, a hymn sung, writing letters to family and friends. Solitary confinement can be an important time for spiritual growth as we study the Bible – and where else does a greater opportunity for prayer exist?

Become what He can use.

For Further Thought ....

Acts 16:25 *"About midnight Paul and Silas were praying and singing hymns to God, and the other prisoners were listening to them."*
WERE PAUL AND SILAS WITNESSES TO OTHER PRISONERS?

1st Thessalonians 5: 16-18 *"Be joyful always; pray continually; give thanks in all circumstances, for this is God's will for you in Christ Jesus."*
WHAT WOULD BE THE RESULT IF A PRISONER DID THESE THINGS IN LOCK-DOWN?

MY NOTES:

Forgiving

"God made Him who had no sin to be sin for us....."
2nd Corinthians 5:21

Have you ever been the victim of unfairness? Have you ever been written up, in prison or in the free world, for something you didn't do? Or, have you been misunderstood and accused of something you never intended?

Sometimes a Rules Violation Report is written on prisoners because an officer is prejudiced, or they've been framed, or they are blamed for what someone else did.

Have you ever tried to appeal a Rules Violation Report written by a staff member? Might as well not bother, right?

If any of the above has happened to you, how did you handle it? It's very hard not to fight it, and it's even harder to not become bitter.

When the innocent Jesus was beaten and hung on a cross, he asked God the Father to forgive His enemies *"because they do not know what they are doing."* What an astounding attitude. What an example of forgiveness and trust in the One who knows the truth.

Built-up anger hurts only ourselves. We are rescued from it when we place unfairness in His Hands.

For Further Thought ....

Romans 5:3 "Not only so, but we rejoice in our sufferings, because we know that suffering produces perseverance; perseverance, character; and character, hope."

Romans 8:28 "And we know that in all things God works for the good of those who love Him, who have been called according to His purpose."

ACCORDING TO THESE SCRIPTURES, DO YOU THINK UNFAIR TREATMENT CAN BE BENEFICIAL TO GOD'S PEOPLE?

MY NOTES:

_____

_____

_____

_____

_____

_____

_____

_____

_____

_____

_____

_____

_____

_____

_____

_____

_____

_____

Regeneration

*"He saved us, not because of righteous things we had done,
but because of His mercy. He saved us through the washing of
rebirth (regeneration) and renewal by
the Holy Spirit..."*
Titus 3:5

Once, after hearing a Department of Corrections official state the need for programs of rehabilitation, a particularly intelligent inmate responded, "Rehabilitation means to return to a former state. I don't think I want to be the crook I was before." He then added, "Regeneration is what I need; to be changed from the inside – and only God can do that."

Programs with opportunities to develop new skills and educational opportunities are essential, but they don't solve the problem of sin.

This example from an anonymous writer says it all:

Let a man go to a psychiatrist and what does he become?
An adjusted sinner.
Let a man go to a physician and what does he become?
A healthy sinner.
Let a man achieve wealth and what does he become?
A wealthy sinner.
Let a man join a church, sign a card, and turn over a new
leaf, and what does he become?
A religious sinner.
Let him go in sincere repentance and faith to the foot of
Calvary's cross, however, and what does be become?
A new creature in Jesus Christ!
Forgiven, reconciled, with meaning and purpose in his life
and on the way to marvelous fulfillment in God's will.

For Further Thought ....

First Peter 1: 3- 9   "Praise be to the God and Father of our Lord Jesus Christ! In His great mercy He has given us new birth into a living hope through the resurrection of Jesus Christ from the dead, and into an inheritance that can never perish, spoil or fade – kept in heaven for you, who through faith are shielded by God's power until the coming of the salvation that is ready to be revealed in the last time. In this you greatly rejoice, though now for a little while you may have had to suffer grief in all kinds of trials. These have come so that your good faith – of greater worth than gold, which perishes even though refined by fire - may be proved genuine and may result in praise, glory, and honor when Jesus Christ is revealed. Though you have not seen Him, you love Him; and even though you do not see Him now, you believe in Him and are filled with inexpressible and glorious joy, for you are receiving the goal of your faith, the salvation of your souls."

THIS RATHER DIFFICULT PASSAGE DESCRIBES RE-GENERATION AS THE NEW BIRTH AND THE HOPE CHRISTIANS HAVE BECAUSE OF IT. HAVE YOU HAD THIS EXPERIENCE?

MY NOTES:

Number One

"Even the very hairs on your head are numbered."
Matthew 10:30

"I advise you to memorize your number, because that is how you will be identified from now on," said the admitting officer in the Receiving Center, to a group of shackled new inmates. The manner in which it was said obviously was intended to mean, *"You are no longer a person. You are nothing."*

What were these new prisoners thinking? Some looked frightened, some sad, some rebellious; one or two even grinned.

The humiliating truth is that the majority of people in society prefer to think of prisoners as non-people, or individuals not worthy of consideration at all.

What about God? While He expects evil behavior to be punished (both in and out of prison), He continues to remember who we are. We are not forgotten and we are never unimportant to the God who made us. If we will but turn to Him in our desperation, we become Number One.

FOR FURTHER THOUGHT .....

"For God so loved the world that He gave his one and only son, that whoever believes in Him shall not perish but have eternal life."
John 3:16

DOES THIS INCLUDE YOU?

Romans 5:8 "But God demonstrated His own love for us in this: While we were yet sinners, Christ died for us."
HOW IMPORTANT ARE YOU TO GOD?

MY NOTES:

The Tongue

"With the tongue we praise our Lord and Father, and with it we curse men ..."
James 3:9

Praise the Lord! Thank you Jesus! Alleluia!
These words, together with other expressions from the lips of some female inmates in a chapel service, warmed my heart. I thanked the Lord for the hands raised in worship and the voices joyfully singing praises.

The next day I came across some of the same ladies as they walked in the chow-line. My Spirit sank as profanity and blasphemy were shouted at each other. Upon seeing me, most of them hushed and said, *"Sorry, we didn't know you were there, Chaplain".*

"Don't apologize to me, I am not God," I sorrowfully said to them.

If their behavior saddened me, how did it appear to God? Did they care? Disrespect for fellow inmates is simply an indication of the much more serious disrespect for the God we profess to love.

For Further Thought ....

James 3: 9-12 "With the tongue we praise our Lord and Father, and with it we curse men, who have been made in God's likeness. Out of the same mouth come praise and cursing. My brothers, this should not be."

"IF YOU CAN'T WALK THE WALK, DON'T TALK THE TALK," WE WOULD SAY TODAY. THINK HOW YOU CAN OVERCOME A FOUL MOUTH OR OTHER HYPOCRITICAL HABITS.

Mark 7: 20-23 "He (Jesus) went on to say, 'What comes out of a man is what makes him unclean. For from within, out of men's hearts, come evil thoughts, sexual immorality, theft, murder, adultery, greed, malice, deceit, lewdness, envy, slander, arrogance and folly. All these evils come from inside and make a man unclean.'"

WHAT MUST WE CLEAN UP IN ORDER TO BE RID OF SINS?

MY NOTES:

_____

_____

_____

_____

_____

_____

_____

_____

_____

_____

_____

Fun

"Delight yourself in the Lord and He will give you the
desires of your heart"
Psalm 37: 4

As I was walking in the prison yard one day, an inmate hollered out to me, *"Hey, Chaplain, what do you do for fun?"* I knew what he was thinking: She doesn't drink alcohol, smoke, cuss, gamble or party. What does she do to enjoy life?

"Everything I do is fun," was my simple answer.

We don't have to run around trying to make fun if we have given our lives to Jesus. The excitement of knowing Him, and the adventure of each day, is sufficient.

We also don't have to force ourselves to give up anything, because He gradually changes our desires to become His desires. Once, when a new believer who was still smoking cigarettes was criticized by a fellow Christian inmate, I reminded them both that God doesn't take the baby's pacifier away immediately. In the book of Ecclesiastes, King Solomon tried everything we consider pleasurable and found it a waste of life.

Belonging to God each day is the most fun of all.

For Further Thought ....

Romans 14:17 *"For the Kingdom of God is not a matter of eating and drinking, but of righteousness, peace and joy in the Holy Spirit."*
COMPARE THE TEMPORARY FUN WE ENJOY DURING ENTERTAINMENT WITH THE PURPOSE-FILLED LIFE OF A CHRISTIAN.

Psalm 4:6-7 *"Many are asking , 'Who can show us any good?' Let the light of your face shine upon us, O Lord. You have filled my heart with greater joy than when their grain and new wine abound."*
HOW DOES THIS SCRIPTURE RELATE TO THE EVENTS IN THE STORY YOU JUST READ?

MY NOTES:

Wise Enthusiasm

*"I am sending you out like sheep among wolves.
Therefore be shrewd as snakes and innocent (gentle)
as doves."*
Matthew 10:16

I always thought of a bull when I saw Ray working out in the gym. He was known to be tough, opinionated, and impulsive. When Ray spoke, other inmates listened. He was the kind of man people would rather have as a friend than an adversary.

I often talked to Ray about his potential for positive influence in the Institution. One day he heard the Spirit of the Lord call his name and he was gloriously saved.

There was immediate and radical change in his focus, but his basic personality and "street" behavior remained intact. He was determined that everyone in his zone would know Jesus.

"Ray, pinning a guy against a wall to make him listen is just not the way it is done," I had to tell him one day.

I admired his zeal, but also had to pray he would receive wisdom to help channel it into a more gentle approach. I remembered and shared with him what a wise preacher once told me: You must be loving and tactful as well as zealous.

For Further Thought ....

Luke 9:51-56 *"As the time approached for Him to be taken up to heaven, Jesus resolutely set out for Jerusalem. And He sent messengers on ahead to get things ready for Him, but the people there did not welcome Him, because He was heading for Jerusalem. When the disciples James and John saw this, they asked, 'Lord, do you want us to call fire down from heaven to destroy them?' But Jesus turned and rebuked them, and they went to another village."*

HOW DID JESUS REACT TO THE ANGER OF HIS DISCIPLES?

First Peter 3:15 *"And in your hearts set apart Christ as Lord. Always be prepared to give an answer to everyone who asks you to give the reason for the hope that you have. But do this with gentleness and respect, keeping a clear conscience, so that those who speak maliciously against your good behavior will be ashamed of their slander."*

HOW CAN YOU "DEFEND YOUR HOPE" WITH GENTLENESS AND RESPECT?

MY NOTES:

_____

_____

_____

_____

_____

_____

_____

_____

_____

_____

_____

Belly of the Fish

"....in my distress I called to the Lord and He answered me. From the depths of the grave you listened to my cry."
Jonah 2:1

Jonah disobeyed God and found himself in the belly of a great fish, unable to help himself in any way.

We often use this story to teach little children the importance of obedience, but they cannot understand the misery Jonah experienced.

We are all guilty of going in a different direction than the one God intended and, at some point in life, we have been forced to cry out to God from what seems like the belly of a fish.

Are you in the fish's belly in one of our nation's jails or prisons? It sure feels like it when you are confined and helpless, doesn't it?

Well, the good news is that Jonah called out to God in his despair and God made the fish vomit him up on the shore.

Jonah certainly was not without scars (can you imagine what he looked like?) But he was once again given an opportunity to do God's will.

For Further Thought ....

Jonah Chapter 2:6 *"To the roots of the mountains I sank down; the earth beneath barred me in forever. But you brought my life up from the pit, O Lord my God."*
GOD RESCUED JONAH. WILL HE DO THE SAME FOR YOU? If you are able, read Chapters 1 and 2 of Jonah.

Romans 10-13 *"For everyone who calls on the name of the Lord will be saved."*

WHAT DOES IT MEAN TO CALL ON THE NAME OF THE LORD AND WHAT ARE WE SAVED FROM? (If you need help, see the last pages of this book.)

MY NOTES:

_____

_____

_____

_____

_____

_____

_____

_____

_____

_____

_____

_____

_____

_____

_____

_____

Serving

"Rather serve one another in love."
Galatians 5:13b

A group of tough-acting, rebellious teenage prisoners gathered in the dining hall one afternoon, listening quite politely as I talked about serving others and one day hoping to hear Jesus say, *"Well done, good and faithful servant."* (Matt.25:23)

The idea of being anyone's servant doesn't go over well in America and especially with young offenders. When I asked who would be willing to serve others, one young man said, *"I ain't being weak for anyone."*

Jesus was not weak. He was strong enough to die willingly on a cross for us. Jesus was equal with God, yet He made Himself nothing and took on the very nature of a servant. (Phil. 2:7)

"I just can't do it," said another. I appreciated his honesty and admitted how difficult it is to humble ourselves.

The only way that any of us can do it is to remember that when we serve others we are actually serving God.

That makes being a servant much easier!

For Further Thought ....

John 13: 13-17 (Jesus said) *"You call me teacher and Lord, and rightly so, for that is what I am. Now that I, your Lord and Teacher, have washed your feet, you also should wash one another's feet. I have set you an example that you should do as I have done for you. I tell you the truth, no servant is greater than his master, nor is a messenger greater than the one who sent him. Now that you know these things, you will be blessed if you do them."*

Philippians 2: 3-5 "Do nothing out of selfish ambition or vain conceit, but in humility consider others better than yourselves. Each of you should look not only to your own interests, but also the interests of others. Your attitude should be the same as that of Christ Jesus."
WHO WAS THE GREATEST SERVANT OF ALL? HOW CAN WE FOLLOW HIS EXAMPLE?

MY NOTES:

_____

_____

_____

_____

_____

_____

_____

_____

_____

_____

_____

_____

_____

_____

Making It

"Be joyful always; pray continuously; give thanks in all circumstances, for this is God's will for you in Christ Jesus."
1 Thessalonians 5:16-18

As I walked around the prison compound, year after year, I often asked the question, *"How are you doing?"* One of the saddest responses has always been, *"Oh, I'm making it."*

That's a typical prison attitude. But my next question, *"Is that the best you can do?"* often made people do a double take.

Is there more to life than "making it?" Should life have more meaning than just getting by?

The apostle Paul often spoke of the crushing experiences of his life: the hunger and beatings, the loneliness of his years in prisons, the illness and frustrations. We forget that he was an ordinary human being. Yet his focus was on bringing honor to God, with a desire to comfort others with the hope he had received.

Just "making it" was not in Paul's vocabulary. He did say, *"I press on....I take hold.... forgetting what is behind..."*
(Philippians 3: 12-14)
He did say, *"For me to live is Christ."*

For Further Thought ....

2nd Corinthians 4: 16-18 "*Therefore we do not lose heart. Though outwardly we are wasting away, yet inwardly we are being renewed day by day. For our light and momentary troubles are achieving for us an eternal glory that far outweighs them all. So we fix our eyes not on what is seen, but on what is unseen. For what is seen is temporary, but what is unseen is eternal.*"
WHAT SHOULD WE FOCUS UPON?

Psalm 33:21 "*We wait in hope for the Lord; He is our help and our shield.* "
WHAT SHOULD OUR HOPE BE IN?

MY NOTES:

_____

_____

_____

_____

_____

_____

_____

_____

_____

_____

_____

_____

_____

_____

_____

_____

Born Again

*"I tell you the truth, no one can see the Kingdom of God
unless he is born again."*
John 3:3

Do we sometimes wish we could turn back the clock;
take a different path; undo the words we said; do a better
job?

Jesus once told Nicodemus, a very important religious
teacher and ruler, that he had to be "born again" to inherit
the Kingdom of God. What he really was telling him is that
there is a way to go in a new direction. In fact, Jesus says
that this is the only way to become part of the Kingdom of
God, with assurance that there can be a bright new future and
an even brighter thereafter.

I often hear the term "born again Christian" as though
there is another category of Christian. Not so, says Jesus.
We are either born again or we are not a Christian.

Nicodemus was quite confused. How is that possible?
Jesus answered that in John 3:7–18.

How do I know when it happens to me? What are the
some of results of being born again?

I no longer look at things the way I once did.
What matters to me (my desires) are totally different.
I do not want that old life – in fact it is distasteful to me.

As long as we live, it is never too late. We must talk (pray)
to God about it.

For Further Thought ....

1 Peter 1:23 "For you have been born again, not of perishable seed but of imperishable, through the living and enduring word of God."
WHAT DOES PETER SAY BEING BORN AGAIN
IS LIKE?

John 1:12-13 "Yet to all who received him, to those who believed in His name, He gave the right to become children of God – children born not of natural descent nor of human decision or a husband's will but born of God."
WHOSE CHILDREN ARE WE WHEN WE ARE
BORN AGAIN?

MY NOTES:

_____
_____
_____
_____
_____
_____
_____
_____
_____
_____
_____
_____
_____
_____
_____
_____
_____
_____

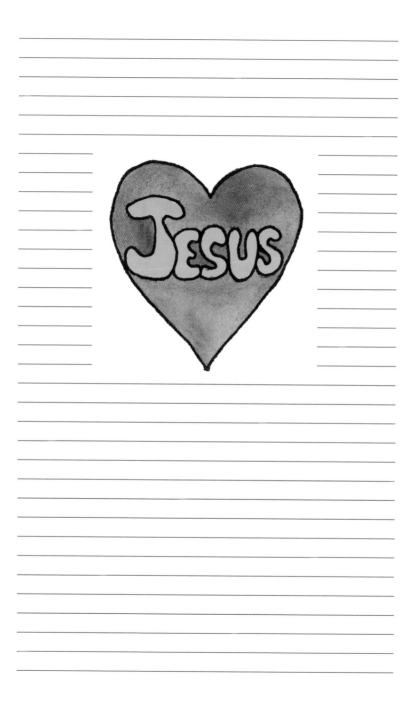

Setbacks

"You intended to harm me, but God intended it
for good to accomplish what is now being done,
the saving of many lives."
Genesis 50:20

Johnny was a Christian inmate, with a perfect prison record, admired by fellow inmates, and liked and trusted by staff. When time for parole consideration arrived, dozens of staff members wrote letters of recommendation, yet he was denied not once, but five times.

In his steadfast determination to live for God in the midst of seemingly endless trials and disappointments, he reminded me of Joseph in the Old Testament.

The cruelty of Joseph's brothers, the vengeance of his slave-owner's wife, the unfair imprisonment and the betrayal of friends, though extremely hard, was God's preparation for Joseph's future of leadership, and for the benefit of a nation of God's people.

Joseph did not become bitter toward those who mistreated him, but recognized that His God uses everything for good to those who love Him.

* Johnny has finally received parole, after serving 21 years. His faith is strong. He has learned much in God's training academy. It will be exciting to see how God will use him in the lives of others.

For Further Thought ....

Romans 8:28 *"And we know that in all things God works for the good of those who love Him, who have been called according to His purpose?"*
CAN WE CLAIM THIS PROMISE IF WE DON'T LOVE GOD?

2nd Corinthians 1: 3-4 *"Praise be to the God and Father of our Lord Jesus Christ, the Father of compassion and the God of all comfort, who comforts us in all our troubles, so that we can comfort those in any trouble with the comfort we ourselves have received from God."*
ARE YOU WILLING TO BE USED TO COMFORT OTHERS?

WHEN YOU ARE ABLE, READ GENESIS CHAPTERS 37, 40 and 50

MY NOTES:

_____

_____

_____

_____

_____

_____

_____

_____

_____

_____

_____

_____

_____

No Compromise

"If the world hates you, keep in mind that it hated me first."
John 15:18

Sue was required to participate in a drug program in the prison. She found herself being ridiculed and threatened with dismissal because the leader didn't want her suggesting that Jesus was the only permanent answer.

When she came to me in tears of frustration, I assured her that this kind of reaction was not unusual from people who don't understand the "Christian world view." I also assured her that persecution of some kind was to be expected because she was no longer a part of "this world."

"What do you mean, Chaplain?" she mournfully asked. I explained that Jesus frequently warned His people that they wouldn't fit in. He even said they would be hated, not because they were evil, but because they were different and could possibly be seen as a threat.

Sue, and all Christians, must strive to keep peace, but not at any price. They must search themselves to make sure they are not being obnoxious, and learn to disagree lovingly, but quietly refuse to compromise their beliefs. If they suffer for right, their reward will eventually be great.

For Further Thought ....

Acts 5: 40-42 "His speech persuaded them. They called the apostles in and had them flogged. Then they ordered them not to speak in the name of Jesus, and let them go. The apostles left the Sanhedrin, rejoicing because they had been counted worthy of suffering disgrace for the Name. Day after day, in the temple courts, they never stopped teaching and proclaiming the good news that Jesus is the Christ."

COULD WE REJOICE IF WE WERE FLOGGED FOR SPEAKING JESUS NAME?

1st Peter 3: 13-14 "Who is going to harm you if you are eager to do good? But even if you should suffer for what is right, you are blessed. Do not fear what they fear; do not be frightened. Always be prepared to give an answer to everyone who asks you to give the reason for the hope that you have. But do this with gentleness and respect."

WOULD IT HELP YOU TO FACE YOUR SUFFERING IF YOU KNEW IT WAS BECAUSE OF DOING GOD'S WILL? HOW?

MY NOTES:

Grinning

"The thief comes only to steal and destroy; I have come that they may have life and have it to the full."
John 10:10

Freddie was transferred from one prison to another. In his former residence he had been involved in all the illegal activities which offenders found available, like acquiring and selling drugs. In the new facility he carefully watched for opportunities to participate in similar practices.

As he later described, he began to notice a steady stream of inmates entering the Chaplains' office and leaving grinning. *"Ah,ha, that's where the dope must be,"* he decided.

On the pretense of requiring a counseling session, he made an appointment to "scope out" the Chaplain's office. He was surprised to find that the smiles he had been witnessing had nothing to do with any illegal activity. Instead he was introduced to Jesus. He discovered that he no longer needed dope to make his life-sentence bearable. He found peace and purpose, in spite of his long sentence and the ever-present razor wire.

He left grinning!

For Further Thought ....

Romans 15:13 *"May the God of hope fill you with all joy and peace as you trust Him, so that you may overflow with hope by the power of the Holy Spirit."*

HOW DO WE OVERFLOW WITH LIFE AND FIND JOY AND FULFILLMENT BECAUSE OF JESUS - OR ARE WE LOOKING FOR HOPE IN OTHER THINGS?

MY NOTES:

Christian Soldier

"Endure hardship like a good soldier of Jesus Christ."
2 Timothy 2:3

The young men in the prison military program listened intently when they were told that to be a Christian was to be a soldier.

"Do you remember singing Onward Christian Soldiers in Sunday School?" I asked. *"Did you perhaps march with a cross lifted in front of you?"* It was fun and it made you feel like a real soldier, but you didn't really understand the significance of living as a soldier.

Now that you have been in this program, you know what it really means to be in the military. You have to be disciplined and obedient and you have to work together if you are going to make it.

You didn't have the privilege of choosing whether or not you would enlist in this army, but you are learning what is required to be a successful participant.

God is looking for a "few good men," who willingly sign up with Him. He doesn't deceive you into thinking it will be an easy catch[1], but the Supreme Commander of the Universe will see that you are trained – and His army is assured of victory.

1. Catch = Job

104

For Further Thought ....

2nd Timothy 2:4 "No one serving as a soldier gets involved in civilian affairs – he wants to please his commanding officer."

THINK ABOUT WHAT MAKES A SUCCESSFUL SOLDIER AND A SUCCESSFUL ARMY, AND APPLY IT TO YOUR CHRISTIAN LIFE.

Ephesians 6:10-17 "Finally, be strong in the Lord and in His mighty power. Put on the full armor of God so that you can take your stand against the devil's schemes. For our struggle is not against flesh and blood, but against the rulers, against the authorities, against the powers of this dark world and against the spiritual forces of evil in the heavenly realms. Therefore, put on the full armor of God so that when the day of evil comes, you may be able to stand your ground, and after you have done everything, to stand. Stand firm then, with the belt of truth buckled around your waist, with the breastplate of righteousness in place, and with your feet fitted with the readiness that comes from the gospel of peace. In addition to all this, take up the shield of faith, with which you can extinguish all the flaming arrows of the evil one. Take the helmet of salvation and the sword of the Spirit, which is the word of God."

WHAT EQUIPMENT DOES THE ARMY OF GOD NEED?

MY NOTES:

Defect or Sin?

"For out of the heart come evil thoughts, murder, adultery,
sexual immorality, theft, false testimony, slander."
Matthew 15:19

I was once interviewing a female inmate as a possible candidate for inclusion in our radio program "Inside Ministries." I asked if she could share her story with me. She described her long-time involvement in theft, from early childhood when she stole candy, to the teenage years when she shoplifted, and finally in her adult years, to breaking and entering for the purpose of stealing anything of value. It eventually led to the sentence she was now serving.

By way of explanation for her actions, she told me *"You see, I have this character defect."* Some well-meaning person had given her this excuse for her "addiction" to stealing. We do the same when we call adultery "an affair" or lying "a little white fib" or drunkenness "alcoholism." Changing the name doesn't excuse us.

"We all certainly have character defects," I told her, *"but the Bible calls them sin."* What she was guilty of was the "sin" of taking what belongs to someone else.

You do not have to commit sin and there is a cure, if you stop making excuses and come to Jesus, and do what the Bible calls repent (being sorry and turning from sin.)

For Further Thought ....

Exodus 20:15   "You shall not steal."
WHAT DOES THIS COMMANDMENT SPECIFICALLY
DESCRIBE?

Revelation 9:21   "Nor did they repent of their murders,
their magic arts, their sexual immorality or their thefts."

EVEN THOUGH THEY HAVE BEEN WARNED, OF WHAT
DOES MANKIND FAIL TO REPENT?

*MY NOTES:*_____

Our Rights

*"But I tell you, Do not resist an evil person. If
someone strikes you on the right cheek,
turn to him the other also."*
Matthew 5:39

Fights are frequent in prisons, particularly in regard to
food. One started on an occasion when a male inmate complained about the portion served by a cafeteria worker.

When a shank[1] appeared, the Goon Squad[2] was sum-
moned to subdue what could easily have developed into a
riot. The offending parties were hauled off to lock-down and
everyone else sent to their buildings.

I happened to be in the cafeteria when this occurred and
I was appalled with such behavior over what seemed to be
a trivial matter. But, it wasn't trivial or insignificant to the
inmates.

How zealously we hang on to what we consider our
"rights." Jesus taught us to turn the other cheek and walk the
second mile. If He means for us to give up a few rights, it is
usually for our own good. In this instance, those involved in
the altercation did not win.

In the end, pride never does!

1. *Shank = homemade weapon*
2. *Goon Squad = security muscle*

For Further Thought ....

Proverbs 16:18   *"Pride goes before destruction, a haughty spirit before a fall."*
Proverbs 13:10   *"Pride only breeds quarrels, but wisdom is found in those who take advice."*
WHAT IS THE RESULT OF PRIDE?

John 12:24   *Jesus said, "I tell you the truth, unless a kernel of wheat falls to the ground and dies, it remains only a single seed. But if it dies, it produces many seeds.*
WHAT ADVICE IS JESUS GIVING HERE?

MY NOTES:

_____

_____

_____

_____

_____

_____

_____

_____

_____

_____

_____

_____

_____

_____

_____

_____

_____

_____

_____

Self

" Do nothing out of selfish ambition or vain conceit, but in humility consider others better than yourselves. Each of you should look not only to your own interests, but also to the interests of others. "
Phillipians 2:3-4

I once visited a girl in Maximum Security who was sitting upon a mattress on the concrete floor, dressed in a paper gown. After telling someone she wanted to die, she was placed in this situation to protect her from herself.

It was certainly not the first suicidal inmate I had encountered. In most cases, I found that threatening suicide was a means to gain attention. The motive was usually self-centered, desiring sympathy for themselves, with no thought for the grief their actions might cause others. Self pity can be devastating to ourselves and others.

Intense concern with self is something all human beings have in common. If we will search our hearts honestly, we will have to admit that even the good things we do often have an element of selfishness: I will be admired, I will feel good about myself, I will receive recognition. I ... I ... I ... !

In a society which is constantly convincing us of our own importance, we are increasingly becoming unconcerned with others.

To a questioning group in a Chapel Bible study group I asked, *"When something happens in your building, say a fight, what is your first thought? Tell the truth."*

One said, *"How it will affect me: Will I be hurt? Will my privileges be taken away?"*

Another confessed, *"Thank goodness I'm not involved."*

Is it possible to do anything devoid of selfishness? Yes, but only as we ask Christ to show us what our motives really are, and then earnestly seek His will in each situation with which we are confronted.

We must see people and situations as He sees them.

For Further Thought ....

Romans 12:3 "*For the grace given to me I say to every one of you: Do not think of yourself more highly than you ought, but rather think of yourself with sober judgment, in accordance with the measure of faith God has given you.*"
WHAT DOES THE WRITER SUGGEST WE DO ABOUT
SELF-CENTEREDNESS?

James 3:16 "*But where you have envy and selfish ambition, there you find disorder and every evil practice.*"
WHAT DOES SELFISH AMBITION CAUSE?

MY NOTES:

_____

_____

_____

_____

_____

_____

_____

_____

_____

_____

_____

_____

_____

_____

_____

_____

_____

Salt

"You are the salt of the earth."
Matthew 5:13a

Not everyone today understands the significance of "salt", but they certainly did in Jesus' day. A person didn't just reach into the cabinet and pull out a box of it. It was much harder to get and much more important in daily life. Perhaps prison inmates appreciate salt more because the food served there is so tasteless. I recall one time when extra salt was not provided on the tables in the chow hall – and the reaction was not pleasant.

In addition to understanding the need of it to improve the taste of food, the people to whom Jesus first spoke these words identified with the absolute necessity of salt to preserve food (they had no freezers or cans.) They also understood its healing powers. (My own mother made me gargle with salt water for a sore throat!)

People who belong to God are His salt. We bring His blessings upon the earth as He uses us to bring His salt to flavor and heal the world.

Perhaps one of the reasons crime is increasing is because many of God's people have lost their saltiness!

For Further Thought ....

*Matthew 5: 13   "You are the salt of the earth. But if salt
loses its saltiness, how can it be made salty again."*

*Luke 14:34-35   "Salt is good, but if it loses its saltiness,
how can it be made salty again? It is fit neither for the soil
nor for the manure pile; it is thrown out."*
HOW IMPORTANT IS IT THAT SALT DOES WHAT IT
IS DESIGNED TO DO?

*Colossians 4:6   "Let your conversation be always full
of grace, seasoned with salt, so that you may know how to
answer everyone."*
WHAT DOES "SALTY CONVERSATION" MEAN?

MY NOTES:

_____
_____
_____
_____
_____
_____
_____
_____
_____
_____
_____
_____
_____
_____
_____
_____
_____

Light

"You are the light of the world."
Matthew 5:14a

In the nightime hours, even from a long distance, a prison appears to be in broad daylight. There are huge overhead lights on poles, and spotlights on all buildings and towers. Even inside the housing units, there is a light on at all hours.

Most new inmates find it extremely difficult to sleep in the beginning, yet they realize the need for illumination to keep down illegal and immoral activity.

When Jesus tells his followers they are the "light of the world," He means they are to expose evil that would otherwise be hidden. But He also means it in a positive way, that they can use it to guide the way toward Him. Our light is a reflection of His great light.

One little candle makes an enormous difference in a dark room. A flashlight can lead us to safety when darkness surrounds us.

For Further Thought ....

Matthew 5:14 -16 (Jesus said) "You are the light of the world. A city on a hill cannot be hidden. Neither do people light a lamp and put it under a bowl. Instead they put it on its stand and it gives light to everyone in the house. In the same way let your light shine before men, that they may see your good deeds and praise your Father in heaven."

WHAT DOES BEING IN THE LIGHT MEAN IN THESE VERSES?

John 1: 4 "In Him was life and that life was the light, so that through Him all men might believe."

WHO IS THE TRUE LIGHT?

Ephesians 5:8 "For you were once darkness, but now you are light in the Lord. Live as children of light."

HOW DOES THE WRITER DESCRIBE CHRISTIANS?

MY NOTES:

_____
_____
_____
_____
_____
_____
_____
_____
_____
_____
_____
_____
_____
_____

Shackled

"I tell you the truth, everyone who sins is a slave to sin."
John 8: 34

One of the most pitiful sights in a prison is to watch a group of shackled inmates shuffling toward a destination over which they have no control. I never saw them without being deeply touched by their total loss of freedom. Did they realize their helpless condition?

There is another kind of shackling which is common, both in prisons and in the "free-world." Those invisible chains of sin that keep us from going in the direction God has for us. We listen to the advice of fools, following a path that only leads to suffering.

It may be many years before we experience physical freedom, but Jesus can free us from the terrible, crushing, burden of spiritual chains instantly, when we humbly call out to Him.

For Further Thought ....

*Proverbs 14:12   "There is a way that seems right to a man,
but in the end it leads to death."*
WHY IS IT IMPORTANT TO DO THINGS GOD'S WAY?

*Matthew 7:13 & 14   "Enter through the narrow gate. For
wide is the gate and broad is the way that leads to destruction, and many enter through it. But small is the gate and
narrow the road that leads to life, and only a few find it."*
WHICH 'ROAD' WOULD WE PREFER TO WALK ON?"

MY NOTES:

_____

_____

_____

_____

_____

_____

_____

_____

_____

_____

_____

_____

_____

_____

_____

_____

_____

_____

_____

Gangsters

*"In everything set them an example by
doing what is good."*
Titus 2:7

Upon transfer to a new facility, I asked the Warden if I could bring two particular inmates from the other prison to assist me in the Chaplains' department. With raised eyebrows he asked, *"Those two gangsters?"* His reaction was not totally unexpected, considering their prior (before Christ) reputations.

After some convincing on my part, he finally agreed they could come, *"But,"* he warned, *"I will be watching them."*

Like the Warden, I have been around inmates for countless years, and the tendency is to be cautious about believing someone in prison who claims to be a Christian. In the past, there were times when what I thought to be heart-felt repentance turned out to be a scam.

The Superintendent did watch for several years and he eventually discovered my "gangsters" were not what they once were. They were, in fact, a positive influence in the prison.

All Christians are being observed by someone. What we consistently live over time is often of the utmost importance to those who are watching us. Our example can mean the difference for them between eternal life in heaven, or hell.

For Further Thought ....

Titus 2: 6-8 "Similarly, encourage the young men to be self-controlled. In everything set them a good example by doing what is good. In your teaching show integrity, seriousness and soundness of speech that cannot be condemned, so that those who oppose you may be ashamed because they have nothing bad to say about us."
READ THESE INSTRUCTIONS TO TITUS AND APPLY THEM TO YOURSELF.

Luke 17:2 "It would be better for him to be thrown into the sea with a millstone tied around his neck than for him to cause one of these little ones to sin."
WHAT DOES JESUS WARN WILL HAPPEN TO THOSE OF US WHO LEAD OTHERS ASTRAY?

MY NOTES:

Deceiver

" And the devil, who deceived them, was thrown into the
lake of burning sulfur ...."
Revelation 20:10a

There are many descriptions for the devil in the Bible.
Perhaps the most telling is "Deceiver." A deceiver is one
who leads people astray, who causes people to believe what
is not true. Some synonyms for the word "deceive" are
betray, hoodwink, bamboozle, and double-cross.

Remember there is not the slightest glimmer of good in
the Deceiver, and his purpose is to keep us away from Jesus
– he doesn't care how.

I told a new volunteer at the prison one day that my job
was "to get people lost." Being an ardent soul winner, he
was quite taken back by that statement. My explanation?
Most of the inmates in this institution are from the "Bible
Belt" and most of them have a church background. They
come in thinking they are Christians because they were at
some point involved in church activities. They have to be
rescued from the false assumption that knowledge of Chris-
tianity makes them right with God.

If the Deceiver can keep us from Jesus by substituting
anything else, even church going, he has accomplished his
evil goal.

Inmates may not have the opportunity to be involved in
a local church, but razor wire and fences cannot keep Jesus
away from anyone who will acknowledge what He has done
for them.

For Further Thought ....

Matthew 7: 15 *"Watch out for false prophets. They come to you in sheep's clothing, but inwardly they are ferocious wolves."*
DOES A DECEIVER LOOK LIKE WHAT HE REALLY IS?

2 Corinthians 13:5 *"Examine yourselves to see whether you are in the faith; test yourselves."*
WHAT SHOULD WE, WHO CLAIM TO BE CHRISTIANS, DO TO BE SURE?

MY NOTES:

_____

_____

_____

_____

_____

_____

_____

_____

_____

_____

_____

_____

_____

_____

_____

_____

_____

_____

Gentle Words

"A gentle answer turns away wrath, but a harsh word stirs up anger."
Proverbs 15:1

The inmate population in a unit housing 1,500 males was suddenly locked down one afternoon. I wondered if it was an escape, or a riot, or a drill. Next came the ERT's, (Emergency Response Team) with sirens shrilling and lights flashing. A number of black-clad individuals rushed into a building.

Bobby Lee had decided he couldn't take it any more and had climbed upon the highest tier and threatened to jump if anyone came near.

The atmosphere was tense and the word "chaos" came to mind as I entered the building with the head of security, with whom I was visiting when the call came for his assistance. The inmates were yelling and the ERT's with bullhorns were insisting that Bobbie Lee come down.

The Security Chief looked the situation over, asked the ERT's to step aside, and calmly said to the terrified inmate, *"Now, Bobby, come on down here and let's talk."* Bobby almost immediately obeyed.

This potentially dangerous situation was diffused by a voice that was authoritative yet gentle. I remember thinking what a difference it would make in prisons, as well as in homes, if we stopped yelling at each other and handled situations quietly and serenely.

For Further Thought ....

Proverbs 25:15 "Through patience a ruler can be persuaded, and a gentle tongue can break a bone." HOW CAN YOU USE THIS ADVICE ? TRY RESPONDING TO ANGER QUIETLY.

Romans 12: 18 "If it is possible, as far as it depends on you, live at peace with everyone." THINK OF WAYS YOU CAN LIVE AT PEACE WITH PEOPLE RIGHT WHERE YOU ARE.

MY NOTES:

_____
_____
_____
_____
_____
_____
_____
_____
_____
_____
_____
_____
_____
_____
_____
_____
_____
_____
_____

Vengeance

"Do not take revenge, my friends, but leave room for God's
wrath, for it is written, 'It is mine to avenge.
I will repay, says that Lord' "
Romans 12:19

One day I went to see 70-year old Annie, who was
locked up in Maximum Security. Earlier that afternoon, she
had been involved in a fight with a young inmate who had
pushed her aside in a chow line. It resulted in Annie biting
off the finger of the teenage offender, and most likely caus-
ing more than a little stress for some security officers.

"Annie," I reprimanded, *"whatever made you do*
such a thing?"

"Well, Chaplain," she replied, *"her finger just sort*
of got in my mouth."

My intention was to voice my disappoval, but her
answer was so unexpected that I couldn't help laughing.
After getting control of myself, I explained God's answer to
violence and unfairness. *"God will fight our battles for us, if*
we will not take matters in our own hands, Annie." With a
sparkle in her eyes, she answered, *"Yeah, but I bet she won't*
bother me any more."

I obviously did not make my point, but the Bible is
full of instances where God fought for people if they were
willing to wait for His intervention. His punishment has a
purpose.

FOR FURTHER THOUGHT ....

Romans 12:21   *"Do not be overcome by evil, but over-come evil with good."*

WHAT IS THE BEST WAY TO OVERCOME EVIL?

Leviticus 19:18 *"Do not seek revenge or bear a grudge against one of your people, but love your neighbor as yourself. I am the Lord."*

DO YOU BEAR A GRUDGE? WHAT WOULD GOD WANT YOU TO DO?

WHAT DOES GOD TELL US TO DO INSTEAD OF TAKING VENGEANCE?

MY NOTES:

_____

_____

_____

_____

_____

_____

_____

_____

_____

_____

_____

_____

_____

_____

_____

_____

_____

Big Hank

*"Wine is a mocker and beer a brawler; whoever
is led astray by them is not wise."*
Proverbs 20:1

Big Hank was a very likeable, capable guy during his years of incarceration. He was probably the best mechanic we had, his talents and pleasing personality being much in demand. Big Hank was an alcoholic and no "program" had helped him overcome it.

Big Hank had, of course, long since lost his family so when he was released he immediately sought out his old friends and started boozing and fighting. He was a regular at the prison.

I remember our many serious talks about his addiction. He agreed that the next time he was released, he would change his friends and not frequent places where he could be tempted. Trouble was, he was comfortable with both, and he wasn't willing to seek God.

Big Hank's latest trip to prison was his last. He died in the prison hospital from an alcohol-related disease.

I was so sad to hear of his suffering. But when I was assured that he had finally called out to Jesus, I felt relief that he was released from the grip of alcohol. His new friend Jesus was waiting for him in a place where there is no temptation.

For Further Thought ....

Proverbs 23: 29-33 "Who has woe? Who has sorrow? Who has red eyes? Those who linger over wine, those who go looking for mixed wine. Don't gaze at wine when it gleams in the cup and goes down smoothly. In the end it bites like a snake and stings like a viper. Your eyes will see strange things, and you will say absurd things."

WHAT ARE THESE VERSES WARNING US ABOUT ALCOHOL?

Psalm 119:9 "How can a young man keep his way pure? By living according to your word."

ARE WE WILLING TO KEEP OUR LIVES PURE?

MY NOTES:

_____
_____
_____
_____
_____
_____
_____
_____
_____
_____
_____
_____
_____
_____
_____

Repentance

"Be self-controlled and alert. Your enemy the devil prowls around like a roaring lion looking for someone to devour."
I Peter 5:8

It was his first time up for parole consideration and "Preacher" didn't expect to make it. To his surprise and delight, the Board agreed to release him because his prison record was beyond reproach and staff members spoke highly of him.

"Preacher" was known and respected by fellow inmates for his Christian testimony and a lifestyle that matched his words. The inmates cheered when he left.

Two weeks later came the shocking news that he was locked up again, having broken into a household. With his parole revoked, he was coming back, most likely to spend the rest of his life in prison.

Disillusioned and condemning inmates had to be reminded of what we must all become aware, that we all have the capability to sin if we do not keep our eyes on Jesus. The Bible is honest about the flaws of God's people. The Bible is also honest about the consequences they paid for disobedience. How sad that we often don't heed.

It is possible to seek, obtain, and accept God's forgiveness - but there is even more. We must steadfastly serve Him and seek to bring honor to His name.

Preacher did repent and he lives today using his failure to warn others. He failed forward!

For Further Thought ....

1st John 1:9 "If we confess our sins, He is faithful and just to forgive us our sins and purify us from all unrighteousness."

Psalm 32:5 "Then I acknowledged my sin to you and did not cover up my iniquity. I said 'I will confess my transgressions to the Lord – and you forgave the guilt of my sin.'"

WHAT IS CONFESSION? WHAT DOES CONFESSION DO FOR US?

IF YOU HAVE A BIBLE, READ THE STORY OF DAVID IN 2nd SAMUEL CHAPTERS 11 AND 12
AND THE GREAT APOSTLE PETER'S STORY IN MARK 14:66-72

MY NOTES:

_____

_____

_____

_____

_____

_____

_____

_____

_____

_____

_____

_____

_____

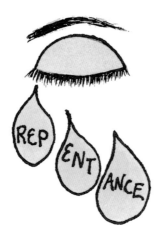

_____
_____
_____
_____
_____
_____
_____
_____
_____
_____
_____
_____
_____
_____
_____
_____
_____
_____
_____
_____
_____
_____
_____

One Way

"Jesus said, "Then neither do I condemn you. Go now and leave your life of sin."
John 8:11

Carol's family was what we now call dysfunctional. Her brother, her hero, slipped out of the house at night to participate in immoral behavior and to sell drugs. She wanted to be just like him. He, in time, inevitably ended up in prison.

Carol left home at sixteen to live on the streets, following in her brother's footsteps. She married a drug seller and they spent most of their time running away from the law. Her crimes eventually caught up with her and she spent prison time in two different states.

Even in prisons there are two kinds of people: those who live in immorality, illegal activity and, therefore, misery - and those who seek to improve and prepare for a better life after release. Carol chose to continue her involvement in darkness.

Some Christian believers consistently visited with Carol in one of the prisons. In the beginning she encouraged them, thinking she could use them. However, because of their teaching about Jesus, their love, and their Godly example, she finally understood that her life did have a purpose. She left her life of sin and began earnestly to pursue good.

When I asked her one day if her family and her upbringing were to blame for her past actions, she replied, *"Not really. They were certainly an influence, but I did know right from wrong. Even though I was aware that what I was doing was wrong, it didn't bother me enough to quit. I had to be told that there is a better way."*

Jesus doesn't condone sin, but neither does he condemn those who repent.

For Further Thought ....

Isaiah 55:7 "Let the wicked forsake his way and the evil man his thoughts. Let him turn to the Lord and He will have mercy on him, and will freely pardon."
WHAT MUST WE DO TO RECEIVE PARDON FROM GOD?

James 4:10 "Humble yourselves before the Lord and He will pick you up."
WHAT IS THIS VERSE TELLING US?

MY NOTES:

_____

_____

_____

_____

_____

_____

_____

_____

_____

_____

_____

_____

_____

_____

_____

_____

_____

_____

Man of God

"But seek His Kingdom and these things will be given to you as well."
Luke 12:31

Larry received a life sentence for a homicide that occurred during a drug deal. Larry was not a drug user, but he did sell drugs in order to buy the luxuries he considered so important.

Educated, with a good job, he wasn't willing to discipline his spending habits, and he certainly wasn't willing to wait for "things."

He attended church out of habit, sang in the choir, and participated in most events, but he led a double life.

When he went to prison, he lost his wife and children, his so-called friends, and all his "stuff," ending up with only a prison uniform, an identification number, and a rack[1] in a building with one-hundred-and-forty other men.

"It was then I realized what was really important," Larry says. *"All I had heard in church about surrendering my life to Christ and trusting Him to supply my needs, became real to me. I am sorry for my past sin, but I am thankful that God forgives, and that I now belong to Him."*

Now out of prison, Larry has had to work hard, but he has regained a family and possessions and, most importantly, a reputation for being a man of God.

1. *Rack = bed*

For Further Thought ....

Luke 12: 22 – 23 *"Then Jesus said to his disciples, 'do not worry about your life, what you will eat; or about your body what you will wear. Life is more than food, and the body more than clothes.'"*
WHAT IS JESUS TELLING US ABOUT
OUR PRIORITIES?

Proverbs 13:11 *"Dishonest money dwindles away, but he who gathers money little by little makes it grow."*
WHAT IS THE BEST WAY TO ACCUMULATE
MONEY?'

MY NOTES:

_____
_____
_____
_____
_____
_____
_____
_____
_____
_____
_____
_____
_____
_____
_____
_____
_____

Submitting

"Submit yourselves for the Lord's sake to every authority instituted among men ....."
1st Peter 2:13

"If my boss-man weren't so ignorant, I wouldn't have so much trouble doing what he says," complained Abby, an educated, articulate, inmate with a long sentence for armed robbery. Being required to obey someone whom she considered to be mentally inferior was a hard pill for her to swallow.

"Abby, Christians are told to obey those in positions of authority over them, even when the order makes no sense to them," I reminded her. *"We must learn to allow God to handle unfairness and stupidity for us."* Even as I said those words, I had to admit how difficult it often is when we are confronted with ignorance.

There was an occasion in the Bible when the followers of Jesus were told by local leaders to "speak no more in the name of Jesus." They did not obey, but they did have to suffer the consequences without complaint.

For Further Thought ....

1st Peter 2:13 –15 "Submit yourselves for the Lord's sake to every authority instituted among men: whether to the king, as the supreme authority, or to governors, who are sent by him to punish those who do wrong, and to commend those who do right. For it is God's will that by doing good you should silence the ignorant talk of foolish men."

WHAT CAN HAPPEN AS A RESULT OF DOING GOOD?

Titus 3: 1 & 2 "Remind the people to be subject to rulers and authorities, to be obedient, to be ready to do whatever is good, to slander no one, to be peaceable and considerate, and to show true humility toward all men."

WHAT IS OUR RESPONSIBILITY IN REGARD TO AUTHORITY?

Romans 13: 1 & 2 "Everyone must submit himself to the governing authorities, for there is no authority except that which God has established. The authorities that exist have been established by God. Consequently, he who rebels against the authority is rebelling against what God has instituted, and those who do so will bring judgment on themselves."

WHO DO WE REBEL AGAINST WHEN WE DISOBEY AUTHORITIES? WHAT IS THE RESULT?

Colossians 3: 23&24 "Whatever you do, work at it with all your heart, as working for the Lord, not for men, since you know that you will receive an inheritance from the Lord as a reward. It is the Lord Christ you are serving."

HOW CAN WE SUBMIT TO AUTHORITY WITH A GOOD ATTITUDE?

MY NOTES:

Tough

"Many are the plans in a man's heart but it is the
Lord's purpose that prevails."
Proverbs 19:21

"Shah" had earned a black-belt in Karate prior to coming to prison. He was tough, admired and feared in the inmate population. He was also charming, handsome and hard-working. The prison staff liked him and he was given a good "catch"[1] as a gym worker. He enjoyed privileges others didn't experience and he sometimes took advantage of them to engage in illegal activities.

Because the Chaplains' offices were in the gym, and because it was his job to be in that location, he was frequently exposed to the spiritual programs presented there.

Shah, somewhat reluctantly at first, agreed to help with some of the big events sponsored by the chaplains' department. I was grateful for his diligence and sharp mind, yet careful not to be too trusting.

One night, with five-hundred other inmates, Shah heard a message of hope from an ex-hippie volunteer who sang *"Tonight is the night."* With tears streaming down his cheeks, he gave his life to the Jesus his mother had taught him about as a child.

Shah had always had the image of tough-guy, but he was not considering his reputation when he publicly repented of his sin.

News of Shah's conversion rapidly spread among the thousands of incarcerated men and women, as he unashamedly became a spokesman for Christ. "If Shah can do it, I can too," was a common reaction.

The tough guy was still tough!

1. *Catch = job*

153

For Further Thought ....

Galatians 1:10   "Am I now trying to win the approval of men, or of God? Or am I trying to please men? If I were still trying to please men I would not be a servant of Christ."

IS WHO WE TRY TO PLEASE AN INDICATION OF OUR SPIRITUAL CONDITION?

Proverbs 16:7   "When a man's ways are pleasing to the Lord, he makes even his enemies live in peace with him."

SHOULD WE MAKE PLEASING GOD OUR PRIORITY?

MY NOTES:

_____
_____
_____
_____
_____
_____
_____
_____
_____
_____
_____
_____
_____
_____
_____
_____
_____

Supreme Judge

"For all have sinned and fall short of the glory of God."
Romans 3:23

If you are in prison, you know what it is to stand before a judge to receive your sentence. Do you know that all people stand before the Supreme Judge, God, and that the sentence is death for all people?

How would you have reacted if someone had said, *"I will take the punishment for you, and you will be free?"*
Jesus did that for all who will accept His sacrifice. He said, *"I came that they may have life."* He took the rap and there is no record of our crimes.

In a human court, someone else would never be allowed to take our punishment. But God did accept what Jesus did for us. The Great Governor expunges the record of anyone who accepts what Jesus did for them. But how do we accept?

1. By believing that Jesus is who He says he is, and that He did die for us. True belief brings sorrow for the sin that made it necessary for Him to take our punishment, and trusting that His sacrifice is enough. We cannot earn forgiveness by doing good works.

2. We must repent (turn from.) Repentance is the word we use for being sorry. We must admit we are sinners. When we are truly sorry, we don't want to continue doing what we have been doing.

3. Believing that Jesus Christ died for you, was buried and rose from the dead.

4. Accepting (like taking a gift someone offers you) is necessary. If we don't take the pardon, it isn't ours.

5. Surrendering (giving up) our rights to do as we please. Unlike the misery we receive when we surrender to the police and receive a prison sentence, we find great joy in belonging to Him and living in His Kingdom, even though it isn't always easy.

For Further Thought ....

Romans 6:23 "For the wages of sin is death, but the gift of God is eternal life in Christ Jesus Our Lord."

HOW DO WE RECEIVE WAGES?

Luke 14:26 – 35 Jesus said, "If anyone comes to me and does not hate his father and mother, his wife and children, his brothers and sisters – yes, even his own life – he cannot be my disciple. And anyone who does not carry his cross and follow me cannot be my disciple. Suppose one of you wants to build a tower. Will he not first sit down and esti-mate the cost to see if he has enough to finish it? .... Or suppose a king is about to go to war against another king. Will he not first sit down and consider whether he is able with ten thousand men to oppose the one coming against him with twenty thousand? If he is not able, he will send a delegation while the other is still a long way off and will ask for terms of peace. In the same way, any of you who does not give up everything he has cannot be my disciple."

WHAT IS THIS PASSAGE TEACHING? (Note: When Jesus tells us to hate our father and mother, He is merely using a term they understood to mean that no person must come ahead of Him.)

157

WHERE WAS JESUS GOING WHEN HE TOOK UP HIS CROSS?

IF YOU WANT TO BE A DISCIPLE OF JESUS, TELL HIM, IN ORDINARY WORDS, THAT YOU LOVE HIM AND THAT YOU WANT TO LIVE YOUR LIFE FOR HIM FROM THIS TIME FORWARD. REMEMBER, HE KNOWS WHEN YOU ARE BEING HONEST.

IF YOU MAKE THE ALL-IMPORTANT DECISION TO FOLLOW JESUS, TALK TO A MINISTER, A CHAPLAIN, OR A CHRISTIAN ... OR CONTACT THIS WRITER AT :

Wendy Hatcher, P.O. Box 270, Glen Allan, MS 38744

Final Thoughts

Prisons are a taste of hell on earth in so many ways, but there is a vast difference. Prisons are not God-forsaken. Neither razor wire or concrete and sophisticated locks, nor cruel human beings, can keep God from penetrating hearts. The Spirit of God enters the isolation of solitary cells and quietly invades the noise and confusion of buildings with hundreds of residents. Those who call out to Him from their desperation are surrounded by His tender love.

We have all seen movies or read books and articles about the depravity in our nations' prisons and they are, for the most part, accurate. In prison society, as in the "free-world," the battle between good and evil rages. I have often told convicts, *"There are really only two races, believer and unbeliever."*

It is always possible to change one's allegiance. On numerous occasions, I have seen the impact which true Christians can make in penal institutions: convicts gathered together in prayer, studying God's Word, learning to obey His commandments; learning to love one another; doing good to those who spitefully use them; seeking to make restitution to those they have harmed; bringing peace into chaos. How privileged I have been to be a part of His people in prison.

Recently while speaking to a group of people, describing the horrors of prison life, a lady angrily said, *"Well, that is just what they deserve."* My reply affirmed that I believe in punishment, but I reminded her that we are all guilty before God, and many of us could easily be in the same situation. In my "Before Christ" days of country-club parties, I used to drink and then drive. How easily I could have caused harm to someone and ended up in prison. And how many of us have been careless behind the wheel of a car or have exceeded the speed limit? God has forgiven us and He forgives the prisoner who truly repents. Can we do less?

Penitentiary Slang

Free-world: anywhere outside the pen
Hit a lick: a favor
Catch: a job
Wrote up: a disciplinary filed against an inmate
New man: a convict who doesn't know his way around
Zu-Zu or Wham-wham: snacks
Rack: bed
Goon squad: security muscle
Shake-down: search by security
Shank: homemade knife
Gar hole: to be trapped or in trouble with no way out
To be on someones hip: to be favored by personnel
Jive: to make false statements.
Snitch: a tattle tale
The man: security
Lock down: an area with no outside privileges
Boss-man: supervisor
Buck: home- made alcohol
Rap down: time to sleep
Home boy: someone from your home town
Weak: someone who can't stand up for themselves
Rap partner: someone you were convicted with
Floor walker: inmate who stays awake at night, cleans
            floors, etc.
Dog boys: inmates working with the dogs
RVR: a rules violation report
Going back: going to the cafeteria for meals
Ace coon boon: best friend

"Ma" Hatcher has traveled with prisoner speaking teams to churches, schools, government functions, etc. for many years. Now retired from full-time work in the state's prisons, she spends her time as a writer, speaker and volunteer. She is available for speaking engagements, book readings, etc., as time and circumstances allow.
Please inquire via e-mail
or telephone:
wendy@wendyhatcher.com
662-839-5784

To order copies of this book, please contact Delta Publishing via e-mail: doingtime@deltaimaging.biz
or visit their website: www.deltaimaging.biz
Orders can be processed online or via U.S. Post.
P.O. Box 25298
Federal Way. WA   98093

For individuals or organizations interested in purchasing books for donating to prisoners, please inquire via e-mail for wholesale prices.